The Inside Guide

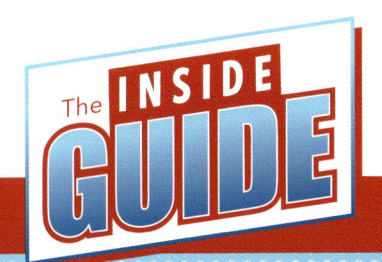

DOCUMENTS OF DEMOCRACY

The U.S. Constitution

By Sadie Silva

Cavendish Square

New York

Published in 2022 by Cavendish Square Publishing, LLC
29 East 21st Street, New York, NY 10010

Copyright © 2022 by Cavendish Square Publishing, LLC

First Edition

No part of this publication may be reproduced, stored in a retrieval system, or transmitted in any form or by any means—electronic, mechanical, photocopying, recording, or otherwise—without the prior permission of the copyright owner. Request for permission should be addressed to Permissions, Cavendish Square Publishing, 29 East 21st Street, New York, NY 10010. Tel (877) 980-4450; fax (877) 980-4454.

Website: cavendishsq.com

This publication represents the opinions and views of the author based on his or her personal experience, knowledge, and research. The information in this book serves as a general guide only. The author and publisher have used their best efforts in preparing this book and disclaim liability rising directly or indirectly from the use and application of this book.

All websites were available and accurate when this book was sent to press.

Portions of this work were originally authored by Therese Shea and published as *The United States Constitution (Documents That Shaped America)*. All new material in this edition authored by Sadie Silva.

Library of Congress Cataloging-in-Publication Data

Names: Silva, Sadie, author.
Title: The U.S. Constitution / Sadie Silva.
Other titles: US Constitution
Description: New York : Cavendish Square Publishing, [2022] | Series: The inside guide: documents of democracy | Includes index.
Identifiers: LCCN 2020043706 | ISBN 9781502660404 (library binding) | ISBN 9781502660381 (paperback) | ISBN 9781502660398 (set) | ISBN 9781502660411 (ebook)
Subjects: LCSH: Constitutional law–United States–Juvenile literature.
Classification: LCC KF4550.Z9 S53 2022 | DDC 342.7302–dc23
LC record available at https://lccn.loc.gov/2020043706

Editor: Caitie McAneney
Copyeditor: Jill Keppeler
Designer: Jessica Nevins

The photographs in this book are used by permission and through the courtesy of: Cover File:Scene at the Signing of the Constitution of the United States.jpg/Wikimedia Commons; pp. 4, 16, 22, 24, 29 (top) Courtesy of the National Archives; p. 6 Universal History Archive/Universal Images Group via Getty Images; p. 7 Hulton Archive/Getty Images; p. 8 Henry Guttmann Collection/Hulton Archive/Getty Images; p. 9 Universal History Archive/Getty Images; p. 10 MPI/Getty Images; p. 12 DNetromphotos/Shutterstock.com; pp. 13, 14 (top right), 14 (bottom), 18 Stock Montage/Stock Montage/Getty Images; p. 14 (top left) Courtesy of the Library of Congress; p. 15 The Print Collector/Print Collector/Getty Images; p. 20 (top) The LIFE Picture Collection via Getty Images; p. 20 (bottom) joe daniel price/Moment/Getty Images; p. 21 Encyclopaedia Britannica/Universal Images Group/Getty Images; p. 25 ak_phuong/Moment/Getty Images; p. 26 Dennis Macdonald/Photolibrary/Getty Images Plus/Getty Images; p. 29 (bottom) Rawpixel.com/Shutterstock.com.

Some of the images in this book illustrate individuals who are models. The depictions do not imply actual situations or events.

CPSIA compliance information: Batch #CW22CSQ: For further information contact Cavendish Square Publishing LLC, New York, New York, at 1-877-980-4450.

Printed in the United States of America

Find us on

CONTENTS

Chapter One: 5
  Challenges and Change

Chapter Two: 11
  Creating a Constitution

Chapter Three: 17
  A Framework for Government

Chapter Four: 23
  Rights and Amendments

U.S. Constitution Compromises 28

Think About It! 29

Glossary 30

Find Out More 31

Index 32

> The U.S. Constitution was written to replace the first constitution of the United States—the Articles of Confederation, pictured here.

CHALLENGES AND CHANGE

Chapter One

The U.S. Constitution isn't just an important document in history; it still shapes our lives every day. Its creation was necessary—the United States faced many challenges after winning its independence, and changes were needed for the nation to succeed.

The Articles of Confederation

The American Revolution (1775–1783) marked the birth of a nation, but the founders of the United States still had a lot of work to do. The former 13 British colonies didn't always want the same things. Plus, they were afraid that a strong central government would lead to tyranny, or unfair treatment, as it had during Britain's rule. Delegates, or representatives, from each state met at the Second Continental Congress in 1775 as the American Revolution began. In 1781, they ratified, or approved, the Articles of Confederation to unite the nation.

The Articles of Confederation were in effect from March 1, 1781, until March 4, 1789. During those eight years, many issues popped up.

Fast Fact
A confederation is a group of states that act together for some purposes. It allows each state to keep its independence.

This constitution gave a lot of power to the states. Under the Articles of Confederation, there was no executive branch, or president. There was no national court system. At least 9 of the 13 states needed to agree to pass new laws. Congress couldn't raise an army and instead had to rely on the **militias** of the states.

Fast Fact

The United States couldn't even pay its soldiers. In 1783, former soldiers threatened to take Congress **hostage** until they were paid.

In 1786, Daniel Shays and 2,000 other farmers in Massachusetts rebelled when they couldn't pay rising property taxes and were faced with the threat of losing their land. Shays's Rebellion showed that the central government had no military power to handle uprisings.

The Congress of the Confederation had no power to collect taxes, and states could decide not to contribute to the national government. The United States had no way to pay what it owed from the American Revolution.

The Constitutional Convention

It was clear that the constitution needed to change. In May 1787, 12 states (not including Rhode Island) sent 55 delegates to the Philadelphia State House in Pennsylvania to revise, or change, the Articles.

However, delegate Edmund Randolph presented the Virginia Plan for reshaping the government and creating a new constitution altogether. The Virginia Plan called for three branches of government (legislative, executive, and judicial). The legislature, or lawmaking body, would have two houses. The number of representatives for each state would be decided by state population. An executive who carried out laws would be

George Washington presided over, or led, the Constitutional Convention. Later, he became the first president of the United States.

OLD IDEAS FOR A NEW COUNTRY

Delegates had to find a workable constitution, so they looked to existing documents for ideas. They used the Magna Carta—a British document from 1215 that made the law a higher power than the British ruler and set a precedent, or model, for fair trials. The English Bill of Rights of 1689 inspired the U.S. Bill of Rights. The convention's delegates also borrowed ideas from **Enlightenment** thinkers Baron de Montesquieu and John Locke. Montesquieu had written about separation of powers, or dividing the central government's powers between different branches. Locke's writings on equality and citizens' natural rights are also woven into the U.S. Constitution.

In 1215, English barons forced King John to sign the Magna Carta, which is shown here.

chosen by the legislature, and a national court system would uphold the law. A system of **checks and balances** would keep any one branch from having too much power.

Up for Debate

What became known as the Constitutional Convention had its share of debates. Some delegates knew a stronger central government was necessary, while others wanted states to keep more power. Some were nervous about a national economic system and an executive branch.

Benjamin Franklin was the oldest delegate at the Constitutional Convention. He was also an inventor, printer, and politician.

One debate had to do with representation in government. The Virginia Plan called for larger states to have more representatives in the legislature. The New Jersey Plan suggested each state should have the same number of representatives. This was better for less-populated states.

Another issue was slavery. Some delegates from the North thought the slave trade should be outlawed. Delegates from the South wanted enslaved people to continue to run their large plantations, or farms. When it came to representation in government, should enslaved people be counted as part of the state population even though they weren't considered citizens? These debates sparked important conversations that shaped the U.S. Constitution.

Fast Fact
Under the Articles of Confederation, each state had one vote on important matters. States with larger populations didn't find this fair.

The Constitutional Convention met at the Philadelphia State House, now called Independence Hall, in 1787.

CREATING A CONSTITUTION

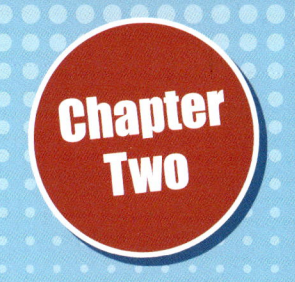

Chapter Two

The Constitutional Convention met from May to September 1787. Delegates debated many important issues and came to **compromises** that would satisfy all the states. Writers constructed a constitution from these conversations, and the ratification of the document began a new phase of U.S. history.

Coming to a Compromise

Several remarkable compromises came out of the Constitutional Convention. The Great Compromise, or Connecticut Compromise, suggested that one legislative house (the Senate) would have equal representation, while the other (the House of Representatives) would have representation according to population. The delegates agreed to this plan.

One compromise forbade Congress from interfering in the slave trade until 1808. Another compromise—the Three-Fifths Compromise—declared each enslaved person would be counted as 3/5 of a person. In other words, every five enslaved people equaled three free people for the purposes of representation.

The last major compromise—the Electoral College—still affects our elections. In this system of voting, a body of representatives from each

THE ELECTORAL COLLEGE

When people vote in a U.S. presidential election, they may think their single vote counts toward a national popular vote in which all votes are counted the same and determine the election's outcome. However, this is not the case—thanks to the Electoral College. Under the Electoral College system, each state gets a certain number of electoral votes. States with higher populations get more votes. Individual citizens vote within a state, and the candidate who gets the most votes then wins all the state's electoral votes. This is the case in all but two states. The states' electoral votes are then counted later. The candidate with the most electoral votes wins.

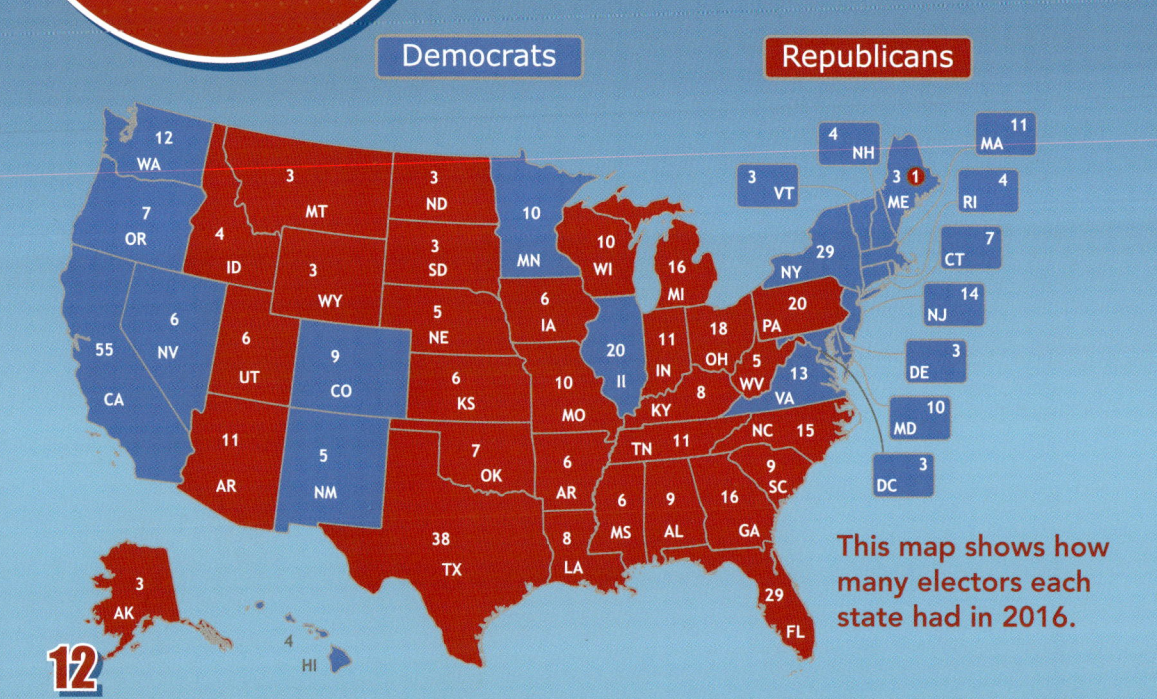

Fast Fact

Because of the Electoral College, a presidential candidate can lose the popular vote but win the election, which happened in 2016. This system angers many voters today.

This map shows how many electors each state had in 2016.

state casts votes to elect the president and the vice president.

Writers Who Shaped a Nation

Several writers impacted the U.S. Constitution, either by writing the document itself or defending it. James Madison is called the "Father of the Constitution" for his role in putting together the ideas in the document. He was the primary writer of the Virginia Plan as well. Gouverneur Morris is given credit for the wording of the document. "We the people" was Morris's choice for the document's beginning.

Americans were still unsure about a new constitution, especially one that created a stronger central government. However, on September 17, 1787, 39 of the 55 delegates signed the document. After this, at least nine states had to ratify it.

James Madison, the fourth president of the United States, has also been called the "Father of the Constitution."

Fast Fact

The man who wrote the actual words of the U.S. Constitution on parchment paper was Jacob Shallus, a clerk who was hired for $30 for his penmanship. He took only a day to write it out, but he made a few misspellings!

The Federalist Papers included 85 essays. They were published in New York newspapers in 1787 and 1788.

Alexander Hamilton

Alexander Hamilton was a vocal supporter of a strong central government. His defense of the Constitution paved the way for its ratification. He was also the first secretary of the U.S. Treasury.

Some of the **Founding Fathers** wrote essays called the Federalist Papers to tell the public why the Constitution was the right choice for the United States. Each essay was signed "Publius," but there were actually several authors. Alexander Hamilton, John Jay, and James Madison

John Jay was a lawyer and statesman from New York. He was one of the signers of the Treaty of Paris (which ended the American Revolution), the first chief justice of the U.S. Supreme Court, and the second governor of New York.

did much of the writing. With their help, the Constitution was on its way to ratification.

Ratifying the Document

There were many "anti-Federalists" who distrusted the proposed central, or federal, government. They wanted a bill of rights to protect against the expanded powers of the federal government.

Supporters of the Constitution, called Federalists, argued that a bill of rights was unnecessary because the Constitution gave the government only the powers listed in the document. However, the Federalists finally agreed to a bill of rights, which would be added later.

This final compromise made all the difference. On June 21, 1788, New Hampshire became the ninth state to ratify the U.S. Constitution.

John Adams, who became the second U.S. president, supported a constitution with separation of powers and a system of checks and balances.

Fast Fact

Rhode Island was the last state to ratify the Constitution—on May 29, 1790, after the U.S. government threatened its trade relationships.

This copy of the U.S. Constitution shows the preamble and Article I.

A FRAMEWORK FOR GOVERNMENT

Chapter Three

The U.S. Constitution set up the framework for the government that exists today. To make sure no one branch of government had too much power, the framework set up a system of checks and balances. For example, the president can veto, or reject, a bill from Congress, but Congress can vote again to pass it. The House can **impeach** the president, while the Senate holds the trial. Also, the chief justice of the Supreme Court presides over the trial.

> **Fast Fact**
> The U.S. Constitution is divided into parts called articles and smaller pieces within each article called sections.

Creating a Congress

The first article of the Constitution sets up a two-house legislature, called Congress. Each state has an equal number of representatives in the Senate and a number **proportional** to its population in the House of Representatives.

Article I explains Congress's structure, powers, limitations, and requirements for members. For example, House representatives must be at least 25 years old, and they serve two-year terms. Senators must be at least 30 years old, and they serve six-year terms.

FAMOUS OPENING WORDS

The opening words of the U.S. Constitution are called the preamble. The preamble focuses on why the document was created, but it doesn't include any laws. It begins with "We the people of the United States," implying that the people of the United States are united as one. It expresses a desire to "form a more perfect Union," which means fixing the shortfalls of the Articles of Confederation. It then promises to work for justice, peace, and freedom, and it commits to promoting the welfare, or well-being, of all people. Lastly, the signers "ordain and establish" the Constitution, or give it power.

Gouverneur Morris wrote the preamble for the U.S. Constitution and is sometimes called the "Penman of the Constitution."

Another section details the lawmaking process. Congressional bills are sent to the president, who may sign them into law or veto them. The many powers of Congress mentioned in Article I include collecting and setting taxes, making money, setting up post offices, forming and maintaining an army and navy, and declaring war.

One clause within Article I lets Congress stretch its powers "to make all laws which shall be necessary and proper" to carry out its duties. This is called the elastic clause. It allows Congress the power to make new laws that aren't mentioned in the Constitution.

> **Fast Fact**
> The Constitution also puts limitations on Congress. Congress cannot suspend "habeas corpus" except in times of rebellion or invasion. This means people can't be held against their will without reason.

A New Executive

The government under the Articles of Confederation didn't have an executive, and people worried that a leader might become all-powerful like a king. The Constitution set up an executive branch in Article II, but it outlined the powers and limitations so that person couldn't become a tyrant.

Article II states that an executive (the president) has the power to make decisions and carry them out. It says the president must be at least 35 years old and a citizen born in the United States. It also explains the Electoral College.

The president has the power and duty to enforce laws, appoint judges with approval by the Senate, make treaties along with the

> **Fast Fact**
> To date, no U.S. president has been removed from office. However, three presidents have been impeached—Andrew Johnson, Bill Clinton, and Donald Trump.

This engraving shows George Washington taking the oath of office before becoming president in 1789.

Senate, and provide Congress with information about the "state of the Union." The president also acts as the commander in chief of the army and navy.

Article II instructs that the president should be removed from office for committing crimes. This is the reason for the impeachment process outlined in the document.

This is the Supreme Court Building in Washington, D.C. Judges, or justices, are appointed by the president but must be approved by the Senate.

Serving Justice

The judicial branch of government is outlined in Article III. The Supreme Court is the highest court in the land. Since 1869, there have typically been nine justices, even if a number wasn't specified in the Constitution.

Justices serve for life as long as they don't break the law. The Supreme Court may hear any case that deals with the law under the Constitution. Article III also promises citizens a fair trial by jury. This was important after the American Revolution, because Americans had been imprisoned without trial or taken to England for trial.

This portrait of the first eight chief, or head, Supreme Court justices was published in 1894.

Fast Fact

Article III also defines treason as declaring war against the United States or helping the nation's enemies, including "giving them aid and comfort."

Congress of the United States,

begun and held at the City of New York, on Wednesday the fourth of March, one thousand seven hundred and eighty nine.

THE Conventions of a number of the States, having at the time of their adopting the Constitution, expressed a desire, in order to prevent misconstruction or abuse of its powers, that further declaratory and restrictive clauses should be added: and as extending the ground of public confidence in the Government, will best ensure the beneficent ends of its institution.

RESOLVED by the Senate and House of Representatives of the United States of America, in Congress assembled, two thirds of both Houses concurring, that the following Articles be proposed to the Legislatures of the several States, as amendments to the Constitution of the United States, all or any of which Articles, when ratified by three fourths of the said Legislatures, to be valid to all intents and purposes, as part of the said Constitution; viz.

ARTICLES in addition to, and amendment of the Constitution of the United States of America, proposed by Congress, and ratified by the several States, pursuant to the fifth Article of the original Constitution.

Article the first... After the first enumeration required by the first Article of the Constitution, there shall be one Representative for every thirty thousand, until the number shall amount to one hundred, after which the proportion shall be so regulated by Congress, that there shall be not less than one hundred Representatives, nor less than one Representative for every forty thousand persons, until the number of Representatives shall amount to two hundred, after which the proportion shall be so regulated by Congress, that there shall not be less than two hundred Representatives, nor more than one Representative for every fifty thousand persons.

Article the second... No law, varying the compensation for the services of the Senators and Representatives, shall take effect, until an election of Representatives shall have intervened.

Article the third... Congress shall make no law respecting an establishment of religion, or prohibiting the free exercise thereof; or abridging the freedom of speech, or of the press; or the right of the people peaceably to assemble, and to petition the Government for a redress of grievances.

Article the fourth... A well regulated Militia, being necessary to the security of a free State, the right of the people to keep and bear Arms, shall not be infringed.

Article the fifth... No Soldier shall, in time of peace be quartered in any house, without the consent of the Owner, nor in time of war, but in a manner to be prescribed by law.

Article the sixth... The right of the people to be secure in their persons, houses, papers, and effects, against unreasonable searches and seizures, shall not be violated, and no Warrants shall issue, but upon probable cause, supported by Oath or affirmation, and particularly describing the place to be searched, and the persons or things to be seized.

Article the seventh... No person shall be held to answer for a capital, or otherwise infamous crime, unless on a presentment or indictment of a Grand Jury, except in cases arising in the land or naval forces, or in the Militia, when in actual service in time of War or public danger; nor shall any person be subject for the same offence to be twice put in jeopardy of life or limb; nor shall be compelled in any criminal case to be a witness against himself, nor be deprived of life, liberty, or property, without due process of law; nor shall private property be taken for public use, without just compensation.

Article the eighth... In all criminal prosecutions, the accused shall enjoy the right to a speedy and public trial, by an impartial jury of the State and district wherein the crime shall have been committed, which district shall have been previously ascertained by law, and to be informed of the nature and cause of the accusation; to be confronted with the witnesses against him; to have compulsory process for obtaining Witnesses in his favor, and to have the Assistance of Counsel for his defence.

Article the ninth... In suits at common law, where the value in controversy shall exceed twenty dollars, the right of trial by jury shall be preserved, and no fact tried by a jury, shall be otherwise re-examined in any Court of the United States, than according to the rules of the common law.

Article the tenth... Excessive bail shall not be required, nor excessive fines imposed, nor cruel and unusual punishments inflicted.

Article the eleventh... The enumeration in the Constitution, of certain rights, shall not be construed to deny or disparage others retained by the people.

Article the twelfth... The powers not delegated to the United States by the Constitution, nor prohibited by it to the States, are reserved to the States respectively, or to the people.

The Bill of Rights is a list of 10 amendments that were added to the Constitution to win over the anti-Federalists who were nervous that the government could strip the rights of its citizens.

RIGHTS AND AMENDMENTS

Chapter Four

The Constitution gives specific rights to states and to individual citizens. This is another safeguard to ensure that the central government doesn't become too powerful. It also allows for amendments to be made to adapt the document to fit the needs of people over time.

Power to the States

Articles IV and VI have to do with state rights and limitations. Article IV of the Constitution says states can make and carry out their own laws. States must respect other states' laws and can't take in other states' criminals. This article also says the federal government will help the states in times of crisis.

Article VI limits the power of state law with the supremacy clause. This declares that the Constitution is "the supreme law of the land." This fixes a problem with the Articles of Confederation in which state laws were so powerful that the central government had little control.

> **Fast Fact**
>
> Article IV allows new states to join the nation, but it specifies that "no new state shall be formed or erected within the **jurisdiction** of any other state" without the approval of state legislatures.

The Bill of Rights

The Bill of Rights includes the first 10 amendments of the Constitution. They were ratified in 1791. These first amendments were promised to some states that were still wary of the Constitution.

The First Amendment gives all citizens freedom of religion, speech, and the press. It also gives them the right to peacefully assemble and **petition** if they are unhappy about something the government is doing.

The Second Amendment protects the right to bear arms (or weapons), while the Third Amendment ensures the right of citizens to refuse housing to soldiers. These were very serious concerns because of England's mistreatment of its colonies.

The Fifth, Sixth, Seventh, and Eighth Amendments give rights to people accused of crimes. The Ninth Amendment and 10th Amendment protect citizens' and states' rights that aren't named in the Constitution.

Changing and Growing

The next 17 amendments made major changes to the country, and some helped make it a fairer place for **minorities**. The 13th Amendment (1865) ended slavery, while the 14th Amendment (1868) made all people "born and naturalized in the United States" citizens. Unfortunately, this didn't fix all **discrimination**. The 15th

This image shows a proposal for the 13th Amendment to the U.S. Constitution, which banned slavery in 1865.

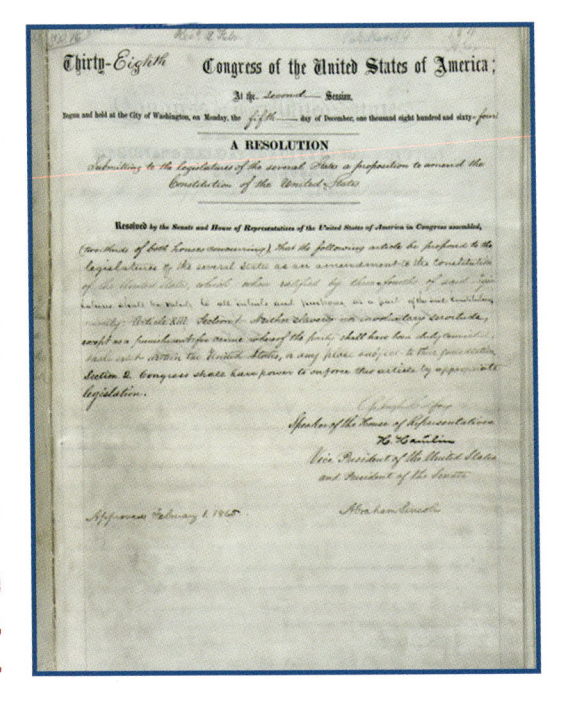

MAKING AMENDMENTS

The Founding Fathers gave the Constitution room to grow. Article V explains how the Constitution can be amended. Two-thirds of each house of Congress must approve a proposed amendment. Then, three-fourths of the state legislatures or state conventions must approve the amendment. Congress has considered more than 9,000 amendments, but only 27 have been ratified as of 2021. Each one is carefully considered by many people before it is made law.

Congress meets in the U.S. Capitol building to make new laws. The House Chamber holds the House of Representatives, while the Senate Chamber holds the Senate.

Fast Fact

The 18th Amendment made it illegal to make or sell alcohol in 1919, while the 21st Amendment repealed, or took away, that amendment in 1933.

Amendment (1870) ensured that people's right to vote shouldn't be denied "on account of race," and the 24th Amendment ended a voting tax that kept many Black Americans from voting. Voting also became fairer with the 19th Amendment, which gave women the right to vote.

The U.S. Senate meets in the Senate Chamber. Senators can sponsor bills, which the Senate can vote on. If a bill passes in the Senate, the House will vote on the bill, and it might become a new law.

> **Fast Fact**
> Our country is both a democracy and a republic. In a republic, people elect representatives to make laws and decisions. A democracy is government by the people, but it can be both direct or indirect (a republic).

Some amendments affected the office of president. For example, the 22nd Amendment (1951) limited presidents to two terms of office, while the 25th Amendment (1967) explained the order in which officials would assume the presidency if the president was removed from office or unable to serve in the position for a certain reason, such as serious illness or injury or death.

The U.S. Constitution that was imagined and written by the Founding Fathers inspired the constitutions of other countries. It's still at work, holding the United States together even in times of struggle. While the Constitution is a big part of our history, it's also a part of our lives every day, as it changes and grows to fit our nation.

U.S. CONSTITUTION COMPROMISES

Issue	Compromise
• slavery	Three-Fifths Compromise: each enslaved person would be considered 3/5 of a person within the population for purposes of representation
• representation	Great Compromise: the upper house of the legislature (Senate) would have two representatives from each state, while the lower house (House of Representatives) would have representatives proportional to population
• voting	Electoral College: a body of representatives from each state (proportional to population) casts votes to elect the president and vice president

THINK ABOUT IT!

1. How did the Constitutional Convention take states' needs into consideration while drafting the U.S. Constitution?

2. Think of a situation in which checks and balances can keep one branch of the government from having too much power.

3. How does the First Amendment affect you as a citizen?

4. Why do you think it's important for the Constitution to be able to grow to fit the needs of a changing country?

GLOSSARY

checks and balances: A system that allows each branch of a government to amend or veto acts of another branch so as to prevent any one branch from exerting too much power.

compromise: A way of two sides reaching agreement in which each gives up something to end an argument.

discrimination: Different—usually unfair—treatment based on factors such as a person's race, age, religion, or gender.

Enlightenment: A movement in the 18th century marked by the rejection of traditional beliefs in favor of logic and science.

Founding Father: A leading figure in the founding of the United States.

hostage: A person who is captured by someone who demands certain things before freeing the captured person.

impeach: To charge a public official with a crime done while in office.

jurisdiction: The limits or territory within which a person or group can exercise authority.

militia: A group of people who are not an official part of the armed forces of a country but are trained like soldiers.

minority: A group of people who are different from the larger group in a country or other area in some way, such as race or religion.

petition: To make a formal written request to a leader or government regarding a particular cause.

proportional: Having a size, number, or amount that is directly related to or appropriate for something.

FIND OUT MORE

Books
Barcella, Laura. *Know Your Rights!: A Modern Kid's Guide to the American Constitution*. New York, NY: Sterling Children's Books, 2018.

Demuth, Patricia Brennan. *What Is the Constitution?* Clive, IA: Turtleback Books, 2018.

Kennedy, Katie. *The Constitution Decoded*. New York, NY: Workman Publishing, 2020.

Websites

BrainPOP: U.S. Constitution
www.brainpop.com/socialstudies/ushistory/usconstitution/
Find fun activities and a movie about the U.S. Constitution here.

President George Washington
www.ducksters.com/biography/uspresidents/georgewashington.php
Learn more about our nation's first executive—President George Washington.

United States Constitution Facts for Kids
kids.kiddle.co/United_States_Constitution
Discover more about the U.S. Constitution, including a list of its amendments.

Publisher's note to educators and parents: Our editors have carefully reviewed these websites to ensure that they are suitable for students. Many websites change frequently, however, and we cannot guarantee that a site's future contents will continue to meet our high standards of quality and educational value. Be advised that students should be closely supervised whenever they access the Internet.

INDEX

A
Adams, John, 15
American Revolution, 5, 7, 14, 21
Articles of Confederation, 4, 5, 6, 8, 9, 18, 19, 23

B
Bill of Rights, 8, 15, 22, 24

C
checks and balances, 9, 15, 17
Congress, U.S., 6, 11, 17, 19, 20, 25
Connecticut (Great) Compromise, 11
Constitutional Convention, 7, 9, 10, 11
Continental Congress, Second, 5

E
elastic clause, 19
Electoral College, 11, 12, 19

F
Federalist Papers, 13, 14
Federalists, 15
Franklin, Benjamin, 9

H
Hamilton, Alexander, 14
House of Representatives, 11, 17, 25, 26

J
Jay, John, 14
John, King of England, 8

L
Locke, John, 8

M
Madison, James, 13, 14
Magna Carta, 8
Montesquieu, Baron de, 8
Morris, Gouverneur, 13, 18

N
New Jersey Plan, 9

P
president, 6, 7, 11, 12, 13, 17, 19, 20, 27

R
Randolph, Edmund, 7

S
Senate, 11, 17, 19, 25, 26
Shays's Rebellion, 6
supremacy clause, 23
Supreme Court, 14, 17, 20, 21

T
Three-Fifths Compromise, 11

V
Virginia Plan, 7, 9, 13

W
Washington, George, 7, 20